SILVER HAIRED SAGE

Retirees Become Amazing Virtual Assistants & Increase Their Own Income

ROBERT J BANNON

This publication is designed to provide accurate and authoritative information in regard to the subject matter covered. It is sold with the understanding that neither the author nor the publisher is engaged in rendering legal, investment, accounting, or other professional services. While the publisher and author have used their best efforts in preparing this book, they make no representations or warranties with respect to the accuracy or completeness of the contents of this book and specifically disclaim any implied warranties of merchantability or fitness for a particular purpose. No warranty may be created or extended by sales representatives or written sales materials. The advice and strategies contained herein may not be suitable for your situation. You should consult with a professional when appropriate. Neither the publisher nor the author shall be liable for any loss of profit or any other commercial damages, including but not limited to special, incidental, consequential, personal, or other damages.

The author acknowledges the assistance of various AI sources in the research, editing, formatting, design, and production of this book.

Book Cover by BookBrush

My mother used to say, "If you don't have something nice to say, don't say anything at all."

I've adapted it.

When you express negative opinions, the Universe will give you more negativity.

Instead, express gratitude and it will you give you more to be grateful for.

Thanks Mom

Contents

FORWARD

Welcome to the empowering world of the *"SIL-VER HAIRED SAGE: Retirees Become Amazing Virtual Assistants and Increase Their Own Income"* – a guide designed to illuminate the path for retirees seeking not just financial stability but a renewed sense of purpose in the virtual landscape.

In the digital age, where experience is as invaluable as ever, your silver hair is a badge of honor, and your expertise is the key to unlocking a whole new chapter of golden opportunities. This book is your companion on a journey of reinvention, where retirement is not a retreat, but an exciting beginning.

Within these pages, we celebrate the unique value retirees bring to the virtual assistant arena. Your wealth of experience, honed skills, and the wisdom accumulated over the years are not just assets — they are the foundation for a flourishing second act. It's time to transition from the familiar to the virtual, where every click represents a chance to not only support businesses but also to enhance your own financial well-being.

Get ready to embrace the exciting prospect of becoming an outstanding virtual assistant, with a goldmine of information and guidance to help you navigate the digital workforce. Your retirement isn't just a time to sit back; it's an opportunity to stand out, to thrive, and to increase your own income in ways you might not have imagined.

So, let's embark on this journey – where silver hair meets innovative virtual prowess, and golden expertise becomes the currency for a fulfilling and prosperous retirement. The adventure awaits!

INTRODUCTION

Greetings, fabulous friend! Ready for the next chapter of your life? Well, buckle up because YOU, the retiree with a zest for life, are about to embark on a virtual adventure like no other.

Forget the snooze button—you traded in the alarm clock for the thrill of a new career as a Virtual Assistant or possibly a highly regarded consultant! Yep, you heard it right. No more early morning rush or endless meetings about meetings. It's time for a new hustle—one that involves pajamas, coffee in hand, and a dash of virtual magic on your laptop.

Picture this: you, armed with a laptop and a twinkle in your eye, ready to conquer the virtual world! From organizing digital chaos to slaying the inbox dragon, you're on a mission to make the virtual universe a more organized, joyful place.

Why the switch, you ask? Well, because retirement doesn't have to be about slowing down; it can be about revving up for the next big adventure! You are here to prove that age is just a number, and the virtual realm is your playground.

Let's make this next chapter of our lives a grand adventure filled with virtual high-fives, laughter, and the occasional victory dance. Who's retired? You are redefining it, one virtual task at a time. Are you ready to join the party?

Chapter 1

BECOMING A VIRTUAL ASSISTANT

A retiree can leverage their experience and skills to offer virtual assistance to entrepreneurs and small businesses in various ways. Here are some steps to prepare:

1. **Identify Your Skills and Experience:**

   ○ Make a list of your skills, expertise, and experiences gained throughout your career.

   ○ Highlight areas where you have extensive knowledge or specialized skills.

2. **Assess Market Needs:**

   ○ Research the needs of entrepreneurs and small businesses. Identify common challenges they face and areas where they might need help.

3. **Define Your Services:**

- Based on your skills and market needs, define the services you can offer. This could include administrative support, project management, social media management, content creation, bookkeeping, etc.

4. **Build an Online Presence:**

- Create a professional online presence. This could be a website or a well-crafted LinkedIn profile showcasing your skills, experience, and the services you offer.

- Use platforms like LinkedIn to connect with entrepreneurs and small business owners.

5. **Networking:**

- Attend online networking events, forums, and groups related to entrepreneurship and small businesses. Engage in conversations and showcase how your skills can benefit them.

6. **Offer Free Resources:**

- Share your knowledge and expertise through blog posts, webinars, or other free resources. This not only demonstrates your expertise but also attracts potential clients.

7. **Set Clear Pricing and Packages:**

- Clearly outline your pricing structure and service packages. Be transparent about what clients can expect from your services.

8. **Create a Portfolio:**

- Develop a portfolio showcasing your past work, achievements, and testimonials. This adds credibility and helps potential clients understand the value you bring.

9. **Stay Updated:**

- Stay informed about industry trends, tools, and technologies. This helps you remain competitive and offer services that are up-to-date.

10. **Build Relationships:**

- Cultivate relationships with your clients. Good relationships can lead to repeat business and referrals.

11. **Utilize Technology:**

- Familiarize yourself with virtual collaboration tools, project management software, and communication platforms. This will help you work seamlessly with clients remotely.

12. **Adapt and Evolve.**

- Be open to adapting your services based on client feedback and changing market demands. Continuous learning and flexibility are essential in a dynamic business environment.

Remember, the key is to show the value you can provide to entrepreneurs and small businesses based on your rich experience and skills. Tailor your services to meet their specific needs and challenges.

Chapter 2

VIRTUAL ASSISTANT – WHO NEEDS ONE?

So, what tasks do small business owners require from a virtual assistant?

Entrepreneurs often have a multitude of tasks on their plates, and a virtual assistant can provide valuable support in various areas. Here are some common tasks that small business owners may require from you:

- **Administrative Support:**

    ◦ Email management

    ◦ Calendar management

    ◦ Data entry

    ◦ Appointment scheduling

- Travel arrangements

- **Customer Service:**

  - Responding to customer inquiries

  - Managing customer support tickets

  - Handling basic customer service issues

- **Social Media Management:**

  - Creating and scheduling posts

  - Monitoring social media accounts

  - Engaging with followers

  - Managing social media advertising campaigns

- **Content Creation:**

  - Writing blog posts or articles

  - Creating marketing materials

  - Developing content for social media

  - Editing and proofreading

- **Research:**

  - Market research

  - Competitor analysis

  - Industry trends research

- **Bookkeeping and Accounting:**

  - Managing invoices

  - Tracking expenses

  - Basic bookkeeping tasks

- **Project Management:**

  - Managing tasks and deadlines

  - Coordinating projects

  - Keeping track of project milestones

- **Website Maintenance:**

  - Updating website content

  - Monitoring website performance

- Basic website management tasks

- **Email Marketing:**

  - Creating and sending newsletters

  - Managing email lists

  - Analyzing email campaign performance

- **Virtual Event Planning:**

  - Organizing webinars or virtual events

  - Coordinating logistics for online events

- **Research and Data Analysis:**

  - Compiling and analyzing data

  - Creating reports

  - Summarizing research findings

- **Tech Support:**

  - Assisting with basic tech issues

  - Managing software updates

- Providing guidance on digital tools and platforms

- **Travel Planning:**

  - Coordinating business trips

  - Booking accommodations and transportation

- **Personal Assistance.**

  - Handling personal tasks for the business owner, such as personal appointments or family arrangements

It's important for virtual assistants to be versatile and adaptable, as the specific tasks can vary based on the nature of the business and the owner's needs. Clear communication and a proactive approach to problem-solving are key qualities that can make a virtual assistant invaluable to a small business owner.

We should note that a virtual assistant does not need to provide all the services listed but can, and should, highlight and offer only those services he or she feels proficient in.

Chapter 3

WHY RETIREES ARE SO VALUABLE

Retirees can bring a wealth of skills and qualifications to the role of a virtual assistant, making them valuable assets for entrepreneurs and small businesses. Here are some unique skills and qualifications that retirees often possess:

Extensive Experience:

Retirees typically have a long history of professional experience in various industries. This experience can translate into a deep understanding of business processes, industry trends, and effective problem-solving skills.

Strong Work Ethic:

Having spent years in the workforce, retirees often possess a strong work ethic, discipline, and a commitment to meeting deadlines. This reliability is crucial for virtual assistants who need to manage tasks independently.

Professional Networks:

Retirees may have an extensive network of professional contacts built over their careers. They could leverage this asset for networking, collaboration, and business development purposes.

Excellent Communication Skills:

Effective communication is a key skill for virtual assistants, and retirees often have well-developed communication skills honed through years of professional interactions.

Problem-Solving Ability:

With years of experience, retirees have likely encountered and resolved a wide range of challenges. This problem-solving ability is invaluable when navigating various tasks and supporting a business owner.

Mentoring and Guidance:

Retirees may offer mentoring and guidance to entrepreneurs based on their extensive experience. This mentorship can be beneficial for small business owners facing challenges or seeking strategic advice.

Adaptability:

Retirees have lived through and adapted to changes in technology, industry trends, and work environments over the years. This adaptability is crucial in the rapidly evolving landscape of virtual work.

Organizational Skills:

Many retirees have developed strong organizational skills throughout their careers. This is beneficial for managing tasks, schedules, and projects efficiently.

Attention to Detail:

Retirees often possess a keen attention to detail, which is crucial for tasks like data entry, proofreading, and quality control.

Calm Under Pressure:

Having faced various challenges throughout their careers, retirees may bring a calm and composed demeanor to the virtual assistant role, even when dealing with tight deadlines or unexpected issues.

Financial Acumen:

Retirees with backgrounds in finance or accounting may bring valuable financial acumen to tasks like bookkeeping, expense tracking, and financial management.

Life Skills:

Life skills, such as time management, patience, and empathy, which retirees have developed through personal and professional experiences, can contribute to effective virtual assistance.

In summary, as Silver Haired Sages we can offer a unique combination of experience, skills, and qualities that make us well-suited for the role of a virtual assistant. Our wealth of knowledge and professional background can bring a seasoned perspective to support entrepreneurs and small businesses in various capacities.

Chapter 4

ON BEING WORLD CLASS

Let's look at what makes you a world class virtual assistant.

A world-class virtual assistant possesses a combination of skills, traits, and qualities that make you highly effective and valuable in supporting businesses. Here are six of the most important characteristics:

1. **Communication Skills:**

   ○ Excellent communication skills are crucial for a world-class virtual assistant. This includes clear and concise written and verbal communication. The ability to understand instructions accurately and convey information effectively is essential for seamless collaboration with clients and team members.

2. **Proactive Approach:**

- World-class virtual assistants are proactive and take initiative. They anticipate the needs of their clients, identify potential issues before they arise, and suggest improvements or solutions. Proactivity is key to providing efficient and anticipatory support.

3. **Organizational Skills:**

- Strong organizational skills are essential for managing tasks, schedules, and priorities effectively. A top quality virtual assistant can juggle multiple responsibilities, set priorities, and ensure that deadlines are met. This includes maintaining an organized digital workspace and keeping track of important information.

4. **Tech Savvy:**

- Being tech-savvy is a significant advantage for virtual assistants. Proficiency in various digital tools, project management platforms, communication apps, and other technology is important for effective virtual collaboration. A world-class virtual assistant stays updated on the latest tools and technologies relevant to their role.

5. **Reliability and Dependability:**

○ The best virtual assistants are highly reliable and dependable. Clients should be able to trust that tasks will be completed accurately and on time. Consistency and a strong work ethic contribute to building trust with clients, leading to long-lasting professional relationships.

6. **Adaptability:**

○ The ability to adapt to changing circumstances, tasks, and priorities is a key characteristic of a world-class virtual assistant. The business environment can be dynamic, and adaptability ensures that a virtual assistant can navigate through challenges and changes with ease. This includes being open to learning new skills and adjusting to changing work requirements. Nothing is worse than someone saying, "well, we've always done it this way..."

○ Don't be that person.

Besides these six characteristics, other valuable traits for a world-class virtual assistant may include attention to detail, problem-solving skills, a positive attitude, and a commitment to continuous improvement. The combination of these qualities allows a virtual assistant to provide exceptional support and contribute significantly to the success of the businesses they serve.

We will go into depth on each of these areas to help you offer the absolute best virtual assistance to your clients:

Communication Skills

Communication skills are crucial for a world-class virtual assistant because effective communication ensures clarity, understanding, and successful collaboration. Here are examples and specific recommendations to enhance communication skills:

1. **Clear and Concise Writing:**

   - **Example:** When composing emails or messages, ensure that the language is clear and concise. Avoid unnecessary jargon and use straightforward language to convey your message.

   - **Recommendation:** Take the time to review and edit your written communication before sending. Consider the recipient's perspective and aim for clarity in your expression. Acronyms may work in some instances but are annoying to anyone not in the inner circle.

2. **Active Listening:**

   - **Example:** During virtual meetings or discussions, demonstrate active listening by nodding, summarizing key points, and asking clarifying questions.

   - **Recommendation:** Practice active listening by focusing on the speaker, avoiding interruptions, and summarizing what you've heard to confirm understanding.

3. Prompt Responsiveness:

○ **Example:** Respond promptly to emails, messages, and inquiries to show your commitment and efficiency in communication.

○ **Recommendation:** Set specific times for checking and responding to messages to ensure timely communication. Use tools like read receipts that enable notifications for urgent matters.

4. Clarity in Instructions:

○ **Example:** When receiving instructions, seek clarification on any ambiguous points to avoid misunderstandings.

○ **Recommendation:** Ask specific questions to ensure you clearly understand expectations. Repeat instructions to confirm accuracy.

5. **Professional Tone:**

- **Example:** Maintain a professional and respectful tone in all communications, including emails, messages, and virtual meetings.

- **Recommendation:** Be mindful of your language, avoid using overly casual expressions in professional correspondence, and tailor your tone to the formality of the communication channel. Double check spelling and grammar. (there, their and they're)

6. **Adapt Communication Style:**

- **Example:** Recognize that different clients or team members may prefer different communication styles (e.g., formal vs. informal). Adjust your approach to align with their preferences.

- **Recommendation:** Observe the communication styles of those you work with and adapt your tone and style accordingly.

7. **Use Visual Aids:**

- **Example:** In virtual meetings, use visual aids, such as slides or documents, to enhance understanding and engagement.

- **Recommendation:** Familiarize yourself with virtual collaboration tools that allow for the sharing of visual content. Use visuals to supplement your verbal communication.

- **Try:** Check out apps like Mural, Google Jamboard, ConceptBoard, LucidChart and Figma.

8. **Feedback:**

- **Example:** Provide constructive feedback in a positive manner, focusing on specific actions and suggesting improvements.

- **Recommendation:** Frame feedback in a way that is actionable and supportive. Acknowledge strengths and offer suggestions for enhancement, sometimes phrasing it as a question, "did you mean...?"

9. **Cultural Sensitivity:**

- **Example:** Be aware of cultural differences that may impact communication styles and adapt your approach accordingly.

- **Recommendation:** Take the time to understand cultural nuances, be respectful of diverse perspectives, and adjust your communication to bridge cultural gaps.

10. **Document Important Information:**

- **Example:** Summarize key points from meetings or discussions and document important instructions for future reference.

- **Recommendation:** Use project management tools, shared documents, or note-taking apps to document and organize information systematically.

According to Microsoft, here are some Project Management Tools to consider:

monday.com: This tool is highly customizable and can be tailored to fit almost any workflow. It is ideal for teams of all sizes and offers a range of features, such as task assignment, scheduling, time tracking, resource allocation, budget management, and progress tracking.

Smartsheet: This tool is best suited for teams with asset proofing needs. It offers a sheet-based approach to project management and includes features such as automated workflows, customizable forms, and real-time collaboration.

Kintone: This tool is ideal for building business apps for your workflows. It offers a range of features, such as customizable forms, automated workflows, and real-time collaboration.

Hub Planner: This tool is best for team scheduling, capacity planning, and requesting work. It offers a range of features, such as resource allocation, time tracking, and real-time collaboration.

By incorporating these examples and recommendations into your communication practices, you can enhance your effectiveness as a virtual assistant and contribute to successful collaborations with clients and team members. Effective communication is a constant skill that can be refined over time through practice and feedback.

Chapter 5

THE PROACTIVE ASSISTANT

A proactive approach is a key characteristic of an outstanding virtual assistant. Proactivity involves anticipating needs, identifying opportunities for improvement, and taking initiative to address challenges before they arise. Here are elements that contribute to an outstanding proactive approach for a virtual assistant:

1. **Anticipation of Needs:**

   - **Example:** If you notice a recurring issue or task that might become problematic in the future, take proactive steps to address it before it becomes a major concern.

   - **Recommendation:** Regularly assess

workflows and processes to identify potential challenges. Anticipate the needs of the client or team and address them before they become urgent.

2. Offering Solutions, Not Just Identifying Problems:

- **Example:** Instead of merely pointing out a problem, provide potential solutions or recommendations to resolve the issue.

- **Recommendation:** When presenting a challenge, include actionable suggestions for improvement. This will require your problem-solving skills and initiative.

3. Initiating Process Improvements:

- **Example:** Identify areas where processes can be streamlined or made more efficient and take the initiative to propose and implement improvements.

- **Recommendation:** Regularly evaluate existing workflows. If you see an opportunity to optimize processes, discuss potential improvements with relevant stakeholders and implement changes with their approval. Be wary of pushback if they don't want to see change.

4. **Staying Informed and Updated:**

   ◦ **Example:** Keep abreast of industry trends, new tools, and technologies that could benefit the business, and proactively suggest their implementation.

   ◦ **Recommendation:** Allocate time for ongoing learning and stay informed about developments in relevant areas. Present new ideas and technologies that align with the business goals.

5. **Timely Follow-Up:**

   ◦ **Example:** Follow up on tasks or projects without waiting for reminders. Provide updates on progress and seek feedback or clarification as needed.

   ◦ **Recommendation:** Develop a system for tracking tasks and deadlines. Regularly check in with clients or team members to ensure that everything is on track and to address any potential issues early on.

6. **Identifying Opportunities for Growth:**

- **Example:** Recognize areas where the business could expand or improve and present ideas for growth opportunities.

- **Recommendation:** Conduct periodic assessments of the business environment and identify potential areas for expansion or improvement. Propose strategies for capitalizing on these opportunities.

7. **Continuous Skills Development:**

- **Example:** Constantly look for opportunities for skills development that align with current or future business needs.

- **Recommendation:** Stay current with industry best practices and trends. Take the initiative to learn new skills or tools that can enhance your effectiveness as a virtual assistant.

8. **Effective Time Management:**

- **Example:** Proactively manage your schedule to prioritize tasks and meet deadlines without the need for constant supervision.

- **Recommendation:** Use time management tools and techniques to organize your workload efficiently. Communicate clearly about task priorities and timelines. Realize that these may need to be changed from time to time. There are many time management tools available online that can help you organize your workload. Here are some popular options.

- Trello: This tool is ideal for visualizing your workflow and organizing tasks into boards. It offers a range of features, such as customizable task views, checklists, and due dates.

- Asana: This tool is best suited for teams with complex workflows. It offers a range of features, such as customizable task views, spreadsheet-like features, and multiple project management methodologies.

- ○ <u>ClickUp</u>: This tool is highly customizable and can be tailored to fit almost any workflow. It works for teams of all sizes and offers a range of features, such as task assignment, scheduling, time tracking, resource allocation, budget management, and progress tracking.

- ○ <u>Wrike</u>: This tool is best suited for teams with complex workflows. It offers a range of features, such as customizable task views, spreadsheet-like features, and enterprise-level security.

- ○ <u>Monday.com</u>: This tool is highly customizable and can be tailored to fit almost any workflow. It is ideal for teams of all sizes and offers a range of features, such as task assignment, scheduling, time tracking, resource allocation, budget management, and progress tracking.

9. **Regularly Seeking Feedback:**

- ○ **Example:** Seek feedback from clients or team members on your performance and use it to make continuous improvements.

- ○ **Recommendation:** Schedule regular check-ins to discuss performance, seek feedback, and ensure that your approach aligns with the expectations of the client or team.

10. **Building Strategic Relationships:**

- ○ **Example:** Cultivate relationships with key stakeholders, clients, or decision makers to foster a positive and collaborative working environment.

- ○ **Recommendation:** Identify individuals or teams with whom a closer working relationship could enhance collaboration. Take steps to build rapport and establish effective communication channels.

An outstanding proactive approach involves a combination of foresight, initiative, problem-solving, and effective communication. By consistently showing these qualities, a virtual assistant can add significant value to the business and contribute to its success. This can be a perilous exercise, however, depending on how and when you offer recommendations for change. Some suggestions might be better received after you have enough experience to know how they will be viewed. You can probably imagine how annoyed a business manager will be if his brand new assistant starts telling him how to change the company during their first week on the job, unless, of course, that's part of the job description.

Chapter 6

ORGANIZATIONAL SKILLS

O rganizational skills are essential for a virtual assistant to effectively manage tasks, schedules, and information. Here are 13 key organizational skills needed for a virtual assistant, along with ways to demonstrate them:

Time Management:

Demonstration: Use a digital calendar to schedule tasks, meetings, and deadlines. Prioritize tasks based on urgency and importance. Set specific blocks of time for focused work and avoid multitasking when possible. This could be a calendar that you share with other team members, if appropriate.

Task Prioritization:

Demonstration: Develop a system for categorizing tasks by urgency and importance. Clearly communicate task priorities to ensure that the most critical tasks are addressed first. Regularly reassess priorities based on changing circumstances.

Effective Communication:

Demonstration: Maintain clear and organized communication channels. Use tools like project management platforms, email, and messaging apps to keep information structured and easily accessible. Label and organize emails and documents for quick retrieval.

File Management:

Demonstration: Organize digital files systematically. Use folders and sub-folders to categorize documents and resources. Adopt a consistent naming convention to make files easily searchable. Regularly clean up and archive files that are no longer needed.

Calendar Management:

Demonstration: Keep an up-to-date calendar with all appointments, deadlines, and meetings. Set reminders for upcoming events. Share calendar access with relevant parties to facilitate coordination and scheduling.

Note-Taking and Documentation:

Demonstration: Develop a system for taking clear and concise notes during meetings or when receiving instructions. Use tools like note-taking apps or collaborative documents to document important information. Summarize key points for quick reference.

Project Management:

Demonstration: Use project management tools to create task lists, set milestones, and track progress. Clearly define project goals, timelines, and deliverables. Regularly update project boards to reflect the current status. Top project management tools include 1. Wrike · 2. Asana · 3. Monday · 4. Adobe Workfront · 5. Smartsheet · 6. Jira · 7. ClickUp · 8. Microsoft Project.

Data Entry and Accuracy:

Demonstration: When entering data, double-check for accuracy and completeness. Create templates for consistent or repetitive data entry. Regularly review and clean up databases to ensure data integrity.

Appointment Scheduling:

Demonstration: Use scheduling tools to efficiently coordinate appointments and meetings. Provide options for meeting times and confirm details with all parties involved. Set reminders to minimize the risk of missed appointments. Some good online appointment scheduling tools include Square Appointments, Setmore, Calendly, Zoho Bookings, Appointy, Doodle, and SimplyBook.me

Inbox Management:

Demonstration: Maintain an organized email inbox. Use labels, folders, and filters to categorize and prioritize emails. Regularly archive or delete unnecessary emails. Respond promptly to important messages.

Adaptability:

Demonstration: Be flexible and adaptable in response to changing priorities or unexpected challenges. Adjust schedules and plans as needed. Communicate changes proactively and offer alternative solutions.

Meeting Preparation:

Demonstration: Prepare for meetings by creating agendas, gathering necessary documents, and reviewing relevant information. Distribute meeting materials in advance. After meetings, summarize key points and action items, and distribute to attendees.

Resource Management:

Demonstration: Efficiently manage resources, such as budget allocation, supplies, or tools. Keep track of resource usage and plan accordingly to avoid shortages or delays.

By consistently showing these organizational skills, a virtual assistant can enhance their efficiency, contribute to smoother operations, and build trust with clients or team members. Being organized not only improves individual performance but also positively affects the overall productivity and success of the business.

Chapter 7

TECH SAVVY

Updating and showcasing tech-savviness is essential for a retiree looking to become a virtual assistant. Here are steps to demonstrate and update your tech skills:

Identify Relevant Technologies:

Assessment: Identify the technologies commonly used in virtual assistant roles, such as project management tools, communication platforms, and productivity software.

Learning: If there are apps and programs you're not familiar with, invest time in learning them. Many platforms offer online tutorials and documentation.

Online Courses and Training:

Platforms: Enroll in online courses on platforms like LinkedIn Learning, Udemy, or Coursera to update your skills.

Certificates: Obtain certificates for completed courses to showcase on your resume or professional profiles.

Build a Digital Presence:

LinkedIn Profile: Update your LinkedIn profile with a professional photo, detailed work experience, and skills related to virtual assistance.

Portfolio: Create a portfolio website to showcase your skills, experiences, and any projects you've worked on. Include details on the technologies you've used. If you need help to create a website, etc. it is worth checking Fiverr for people with the correct tech skills. Unless, of course, this is a skill you want to build for yourself, in which case, you might open a whole new business opportunity.

Highlight Tech Skills on Resume:

Skills Section: Include a dedicated skills section on your resume, highlighting your tech skills.

Relevant Experience: In your experience section, mention any tech-related tasks you've performed in previous roles.

Stay Current with Trends:

News and Blogs: Regularly read tech news and blogs to stay informed about the latest trends and tools in the virtual assistant space.

Networking: Join online forums or communities related to virtual assistance to discuss and learn about new technologies.

Showcase Tech Projects:

Portfolio: If you've worked on tech-related projects, showcase them in your portfolio. Provide details about your role, the technologies used, and the outcomes.

Case Studies: Create case studies for significant projects, explaining the challenges faced and the solutions implemented.

Use Tech Tools in Your Work:

Integration: Integrate tech tools into your daily work, such as project management platforms, communication apps, or collaboration tools.

Efficiency: Demonstrate how the use of technology has improved your efficiency and contributed to successful outcomes in your previous roles.

Online Presence and Networking:

LinkedIn Groups: Join LinkedIn groups related to virtual assistance, technology, or specific tools. Engage in discussions to increase and showcase your knowledge.

Social Media: Use social media platforms to share insights, articles, and updates about relevant technologies.

Create How-To Content:

Blog Posts or Videos: Share your knowledge by creating how-to blog posts or videos related to virtual assistance or specific technologies.

Webinars: Host webinars on topics you are knowledgeable about, showcasing your expertise.

Seek Recommendations:

LinkedIn Recommendations: Request recommendations from colleagues, supervisors, or clients who can speak to your tech skills and proficiency.

Testimonials: If you've worked on projects, ask clients for testimonials that highlight your tech-savvy contributions.

Online Presence in Relevant Platforms:

GitHub or GitLab: If relevant to your work, consider creating a GitHub or GitLab account to showcase code, scripts, or projects.

Professional Networks:

Establish a presence on professional networks such as Behance, Dribbble, or others that align with your skills.

Artificial Intelligence:

AI tools can help virtual assistants perform a variety of tasks more efficiently. Here are some examples:

Task management: AI-powered task management tools like Taskade and ClickUp can help you prioritize tasks more effectively by using natural language processing, machine learning, and predictive analytics to identify the best order in which to complete tasks and offer suggestions accordingly.

Workflow automation: AI can help automate repetitive tasks and workflows, freeing up time for virtual assistants to focus on more complex tasks. Tools like Kintone and Taskade offer features such as customizable forms, automated workflows, and real-time collaboration to help streamline your workflow.

Data analysis: AI can help assistants analyze large amounts of data more quickly and accurately. Tools like Smartsheet offer features such as automated workflows, customizable forms, and real-time collaboration to help you manage your data more effectively.

Scheduling: AI-powered scheduling tools like Hub Planner can help you manage your schedule more effectively by offering features such as resource allocation, time tracking, and real-time collaboration.

These are just a few examples of how AI tools can help virtual assistants perform their tasks. The biggest area of help that AI can provide is in research. If you employ Chat GPT, Bing Chat or any other AI tool, please remember that these kids require adult supervision. That would be you. Don't assume that the information they present is always accurate. Corroborate it.

By taking these steps, a retiree can effectively update and showcase their tech-savvy skills to potential virtual assistant clients. Continuous learning, practical application, and a strong online presence will contribute to a compelling profile that reflects proficiency in relevant technologies.

Chapter 8

RELIABILITY AND DEPENDABILITY

D emonstrating reliability and dependability is crucial for someone seeking to establish themselves as a trustworthy virtual assistant. Here are ways a retiree can showcase these qualities:

1. **Consistent Communication:**

   ○ **Timely Responses:** Respond promptly to emails, messages, and communication from clients or team members. Establish a communication routine to keep stakeholders informed about your availability.

2. **Clear Expectations:**

   ○ **Setting Expectations:** Clearly communicate your working hours, response times, and any potential time off in advance. Manage expectations regarding your availability and deadlines.

3. **Adherence to Deadlines:**

- **Task Completion:** Consistently meet or exceed deadlines for tasks and projects. Provide updates on the progress of ongoing work and communicate proactively if there are any potential delays.

4. **Task Prioritization:**

- **Prioritize Effectively:** Demonstrate an ability to prioritize tasks based on urgency and importance. Ensure that critical tasks are completed on time, even in the face of competing demands.

5. **Reliable Systems and Processes:**

- **Consistent Workflow:** Develop and maintain reliable systems and processes for task management, project coordination, and communication. Consistency in your approach contributes to predictability.

6. Professionalism in Communication:

- **Respectful Tone:** Maintain a professional and respectful tone in all written and verbal communications. Be courteous and considerate when interacting with clients, team members, or stakeholders.

7. Transparent Updates:

- **Regular Updates:** Provide regular updates on the status of ongoing projects. Share progress reports, milestones achieved, and any potential challenges. Transparency builds trust.

8. Emergency Planning:

- **Contingency Plans:** Have contingency plans in place for unexpected events or emergencies that may affect your availability. Communicate these plans to clients and stakeholders in advance.

9. Accountability:

- **Owning Mistakes:** If mistakes occur,

take accountability for them, communicate openly, and present solutions to rectify the situation. Demonstrating responsibility during challenging times reinforces dependability.

10. **Consistent Quality of Work:**

- **High Standards:** Uphold high standards for the quality of your work. Consistently deliver work that meets or exceeds expectations. A track record of quality work builds trust.

11. **Reliable Technology Use:**

- **Tech Maintenance:** Ensure that your technology tools are reliable and well-maintained. Regularly update software, backup data, and troubleshoot any issues promptly to minimize disruptions.

12. **Dependable in Remote Work:**

- **Remote Collaboration:** Showcase your ability to work effectively in a remote environment. Use virtual collaboration tools

proficiently and maintain consistent productivity.

13. **Adherence to Confidentiality:**

- ○ **Respecting Privacy:** Demonstrate a commitment to confidentiality and privacy. Respect sensitive information and adhere to
  any confidentiality agreements in place.
  You have no idea who is standing behind
  you in the cashier line while you are gos-
  siping about a company or person.

- ○ This is especially important if you have
  more than one client at a time. It would
  be extremely unprofessional, and possibly
  illegal, to offer proprietary information between companies.

14. **Seek Feedback:**

- ○ **Continuous Improvement:** Actively seek
  feedback from clients and team members.
  Use feedback to identify areas for improvement and show a commitment to continuous growth and refinement.

By consistently embodying these qualities, a retiree can establish themselves as a reliable and dependable virtual assistant. Building trust through clear communication, consistent performance, and a commitment to professionalism is key to success in this role.

Chapter 9

ADAPTABILITY

Showcasing adaptability on a profile is important for a retiree seeking to become a virtual assistant. Here are specific ways to highlight adaptability in your profile:

1. **Include a Section on Adaptability:**

   - **Profile Introduction:** Begin your profile with a brief introduction that explicitly mentions your adaptability and flexibility in handling diverse tasks and challenges.

2. **Highlight Diverse Experience:**

   - **Work History:** Detail your diverse work experience, emphasizing roles that required adaptability. Mention instances where you successfully navigated change, learned new skills, or took on new responsibilities.

3. **Skillset Section:**

- **Adaptable Skills:** In your skills section, include traits such as "Adaptability," "Flexibility," and "Versatility." List specific skills you've gained over the years that show your ability to adapt to different tasks and technologies.

4. **Showcase Learning Experiences:**

- **Continuous Learning:** Mention any courses, certifications, or workshops you've undertaken to stay updated in your field or learn new skills. This reflects a proactive approach to adaptability.

5. **Case Studies and Projects:**

- **Highlight Challenges:** In your portfolio or work history, include case studies or projects where you faced challenges and adapted your approach to achieve successful outcomes.

6. **Emphasize Industry Changes:**

- **Industry Evolution:** If relevant, discuss how you've navigated changes in your industry over the years. Mention any transformations you witnessed and adapted to during your professional journey.

7. **Highlight Technology Adoption:**

- **Tech Integration:** If you've embraced new technologies throughout your career, showcase this. Discuss instances where you successfully implemented new tools or adapted to changes in technology.

8. **Address Work Environment Changes:**

- **Remote Work Experience:** If you have experience working remotely or adapting to different work environments, highlight this. Remote work showcases adaptability to changing work trends. You can reference any accommodations that you made during the pandemic of 2021-22, for instance.

9. **Problem-Solving Success Stories:**

○ **Case Studies:** Share stories of problem-solving where your adaptability played a crucial role. Discuss how you approached challenges, adjusted strategies, and achieved positive outcomes.

10. **Soft Skills Emphasis:**

○ **Soft Skills Section:** Include a section on soft skills, emphasizing attributes like resilience, open-mindedness, and the ability to thrive in dynamic work environments.

11. **Volunteer or Side Projects:**

○ **Diverse Projects:** If you've taken on volunteer work or side projects, discuss how these experiences allowed you to adapt to different contexts and contribute your skills in various ways.

12. **Client Testimonials:**

○ **Adaptability Endorsements:** If possible, seek client testimonials that specifically highlight your adaptability. Clients can provide insights into how you've adjusted to their unique needs and challenges.

13. **Continuous Improvement Mentality:**

- **Professional Development:** Express a commitment to ongoing professional development and improvement. This signals to potential clients that you're proactive about staying adaptable in a rapidly changing professional landscape.

Remember to weave these elements into the narrative of your profile, providing concrete examples and anecdotes to support your claims of adaptability. By doing so, you'll present a compelling case for your ability to navigate diverse challenges and contribute effectively as a virtual assistant.

If you need to highlight continuing education but wonder about the costs and time commitments, look at some of the free classes offered by many major universities. A certificate from an Ivy League college will give credibility to your efforts to stay current.

Many of the key elements of the preceding outstanding characteristics of a world class virtual assistant may sound repetitive but look carefully and implement them in your profile. Their repetitiveness simply shows how important they are to your success as an outstanding and in demand virtual assistant.

Chapter 10

WHY THEY NEED YOU

Let your prospective client meet a seasoned professional with a passport stamped full of experience and a knack for turning virtual chaos into organized bliss!

Experience Extravaganza: With more professional years under your belt than a birthday cake wants to count, you bring a truckload of experience. From conquering the fax machine era to Zooming through virtual meetings, you've seen it all.

Time Traveler GOAT: Armed with a time-turner (or at least, excellent time management skills), you defy the laws of procrastination. Deadlines? Pfft, you mastered the art of getting things done yesterday!

Tech Extraordinaire: While some might think cloudy refers to the ones in the sky, you are a tech-savvy wizard. From floppy disks to cloud storage, you have seamlessly glided through the digital evolution.

The Juggler: Not just another circus act! You can juggle more tasks than a clown with a bag full of rubber chickens. From scheduling to project management, you keep more balls in the air than a magician at a talent show.

Adaptability All-Star: Changing faster than the weather? It's not an issue for you. You've weathered many storms and embraced change like a long-lost friend. Through it all, you still managed to keep a smile on your face.

Master of All Trades: Need someone to fix an Excel formula, plan a virtual party, and manage a project? You are the Swiss army knife of virtual assistants. No task is too big, no challenge too small!

Communication Maestro: If effective communication was an instrument, you would be a virtuoso. Emails, phone calls, carrier pigeons—you've mastered them all. They will never have to wonder, "Where in the world is Waldo or,[Your Name]?"

Positive Vibes Only: Forget rainbows; you bring positivity wherever you go. A virtual ray of sunshine, you turn even the dreariest tasks into opportunities for joy.

So, if a company needs the wisdom of Yoda, the organizational skills of Marie Kondo, and the adaptability of a chameleon at a disco, look no further! You are not just a virtual assistant; you are the superhero their world needs.

Chapter 11

VA REVIEW

A quick review of what a retiree needs in order to be a world class virtual assistant:

1. Virtual Assistance from Retirees:

• Retirees can leverage their experience, skills, and adaptability to pursue a new career as virtual assistants for entrepreneurs and small businesses.

2. Tasks by Virtual Assistants:

• Virtual assistants can handle various tasks, including administrative duties, customer support, social media management, and more, to support the efficient operation of businesses.

3. Unique Skills of Retirees as Virtual Assistants:

• Retirees bring valuable qualities such as experience, maturity, a strong work ethic, reliability, and a broad skill set to the role of virtual assistant.

4. Differences Between Virtual Assistants and Consultants:

• Virtual assistants focus on day-to-day operational tasks, while consultants offer specialized expertise, strategic advice, and project-based solutions to address broader business challenges.

5. Characteristics of a World-Class Virtual Assistant:

• World-class virtual assistants possess communication skills, a proactive approach, organizational skills, tech savviness, reliability, dependability, adaptability, and a commitment to continuous improvement.

6. Communication Skills:

• Clear and concise writing, active listening, prompt responsiveness, clarity in instructions, and effective use of visual aids are crucial components of excellent communication skills for virtual assistants.

7. Organizational Skills:

• Time management, task prioritization, effective communication, file and project management, and adaptability are key organizational skills that virtual assistants should demonstrate.

8. Adaptability Showcase for Retirees:

• Retirees can showcase adaptability by highlighting diverse experiences, emphasizing continuous learning, sharing success stories of navigating change, and addressing how they've embraced technology and remote work.

9. Reliability and Dependability:

• Virtual assistants, including retirees, can show reliability by maintaining consistent communication, setting clear expectations, adhering to deadlines, prioritizing tasks, and being accountable for their work.

10. Profile Building for Tech Savvy Retirees:

• Retirees can update their profiles by showcasing tech-savvy skills through online courses, a digital presence, highlighting tech-related projects, staying current with trends, and seeking recommendations.

11. Introduction for Retirees as Virtual Assistants:

• A retiree entering the virtual assistant world can present themselves as an experienced, adaptable, and tech-savvy professional, ready to bring a wealth of skills to tackle tasks with enthusiasm and positivity.

12. Key Attributes for a World-Class Virtual Assistant:

• Experience, time management, tech-savviness, adaptability, and a positive attitude are essential attributes for a retiree aiming to become a world-class virtual assistant.

13. Retiree's Next Chapter as a Virtual Assistant:

• The transition to a virtual assistant role for retirees is framed as an exciting encore adventure, leveraging experience, adaptability, and a knack for organization to contribute to the virtual realm with positivity and enthusiasm.

Chapter 12

FINDING OPPORTUNITIES

Now that we know what it takes to be an outstanding virtual assistant, where can we go to find such an interesting position?

Check online sites like:

Upwork: Upwork is a popular freelancing platform where businesses and individuals post virtual assistant jobs. You can create a profile, highlight your skills and experience, and bid on relevant projects.

Fiverr: Fiverr is another freelancing platform where you can create "gigs" offering your virtual assistant services. Clients can then hire you based on your profile and gig descriptions.

Freelancer: Freelancer is a global freelancing platform similar to Upwork. You can create a profile, bid on projects, and connect with potential clients seeking virtual assistants.

Remote.co: Remote.co lists remote jobs in various categories, including virtual assistant positions. You can search for part-time opportunities that match your skills and preferences.

FlexJobs: FlexJobs specializes in flexible and remote work opportunities. It requires a subscription, but it screens job listings to ensure they are legitimate and high-quality.

In addition, here are some more places to look:

LinkedIn

Monster

Indeed

Robert Half

Zip Recruiter

TaskRabbit

Chapter 13

CONSULTANTS VS. ASSISTANTS

M any people retire from a job or profession and move into a consultant role with their former employer or offer their services to other members of their profession. Let's look at the similarities and differences between "virtual assistants" and "consultants."

Virtual assistants and consultants are both professionals who provide support and expertise to businesses, but they differ in their roles, functions, and the nature of their relationships with clients. Here are the key differences and similarities between a virtual assistant and a consultant.

Differences:

   1. **Scope of Work:**

- **Virtual Assistant (VA):** VA's typically handle administrative and operational tasks such as email management, scheduling, data entry, and customer support. Their focus is on providing day-to-day support to streamline business operations.

- **Consultant:** Consultants are hired for their specialized expertise in a particular field. They often provide strategic advice, conduct assessments, and offer solutions to specific business challenges. Consultants focus on addressing broader business issues and opportunities.

2. **Level of Expertise:**

- **Virtual Assistant (VA):** VA's usually have a diverse skill set and may handle a range of tasks. While they are skilled professionals, their expertise is often more generalized and focused on operational efficiency.

- **Consultant:** Consultants are specialists in a specific domain or industry. They bring in-depth knowledge and experience to address complex problems, make strategic decisions, and provide high-level guidance.

3. Duration of Engagement:

- **Virtual Assistant (VA):** VA's often have on-going, long-term relationships with clients to provide consistent support in daily operations. The engagement is more continuous and may involve routine tasks.

- **Consultant:** Consultant engagements are often project-based and may have a specific duration. They are brought in for a defined period to work on a particular issue or initiative.

4. Task-Oriented vs. Strategic Focus.

- **Virtual Assistant (VA):** VA's focus on executing tasks efficiently and may not be primarily involved in strategic decision-making. Their role is to handle routine functions to free up time for business owners and managers.

- **Consultant:** Consultants are hired for

their strategic thinking. They analyze business challenges, develop plans, and provide recommendations that can affect the overall direction and success of the business.

Similarities:

1. **Remote Work:**

- Both virtual assistants and consultants can usually work remotely, providing their services without the need to always be physically present at the client's location. This is especially common in today's digital age.

2. **Client Collaboration:**

- Both professionals collaborate closely with clients to understand their needs, goals, and challenges. Effective communication and a strong client-provider relationship are essential for success.

3. **Client-Centric Approach:**

- Whether a virtual assistant or a consultant, both roles are centered on meeting the needs of the client. They aim to add value and contribute to the success of the businesses they serve.

4. **Professionalism:**

- Both virtual assistants and consultants are expected to maintain a high level of professionalism in their interactions with clients. This includes reliability, confidentiality, and ethical conduct.

In summary, while virtual assistants and consultants share some similarities, such as remote work capabilities and a client-centric approach, their differences lie in the scope of work, level of expertise, duration of engagement, and focus on tasks versus strategic initiatives. Each role serves a unique purpose in supporting businesses based on their specific needs and challenges.

Chapter 14

ONLINE CONSULTING

Offering online consulting services can be a rewarding endeavor for retirees. Here are some main points to consider:

1. **Identify Expertise:**

   ○ Leverage your professional background, skills, and expertise gained throughout your career to offer valuable consulting services.

2. **Choose a Niche:**

   ○ Narrow down your focus to a specific niche or industry where you can provide specialized knowledge and guidance.

3. **Online Presence:**

- Establish a professional online presence through a website or social media, like LinkedIn, to showcase your expertise and services.

4. **Set Clear Offerings:**

- Clearly define the consulting services you offer. Outline specific deliverables, consultation packages, and pricing structures.

5. **Digital Communication Tools:**

- Familiarize yourself with digital communication tools like video conferencing, email, and project management platforms to interact with clients effectively.

6. **Create a Portfolio:**

- Develop a portfolio highlighting your achievements, case studies, and successful projects to build credibility with potential clients. You might need to lean on your previous employment experience to get started.

7. **Pricing Strategy:**

- ◦ Determine a fair and competitive pricing strategy for your consulting services. Consider hourly rates, project-based pricing, or retainer models.

8. **Client Onboarding Process:**

- ◦ Establish a smooth onboarding process for new clients. Clearly communicate your consulting approach, expectations, and the steps involved in working together.

9. **Legal Considerations:**

- ◦ Understand and address legal considerations, such as contracts, confidentiality agreements, and any industry-specific regulations. You might be required to sign a Non-Disclosure agreement. Be sure to understand its terms.

10. **Marketing and Networking:**

- ◦ Actively market your consulting services through online channels, social media, and industry forums.

○ Network with professionals in your niche to expand your reach and gain referrals.

11. Continued Learning:

○ Stay updated with industry trends and advancements. Continuous learning ensures your consulting services remain relevant and valuable.

12. Client Relationship Management:

○ Foster strong relationships with clients. Regular communication, feedback sessions, and personalized attention contribute to client satisfaction.

13. Time Management:

○ Efficiently manage your time to balance consulting work with other aspects of retirement life. Clearly define work hours and boundaries.

14. Offer Free Resources:

- Provide free resources, such as blog posts, webinars, or whitepapers, to showcase your expertise and attract potential clients. A well-written e-book that you could distribute to potential clients showcasing your expertise is a very professional way to promote yourself.

15. Feedback and Improvement:

- Seek feedback from clients to understand areas for improvement. Use this feedback to enhance your consulting services and refine your approach.

16. Build a Referral Network:

- Encourage satisfied clients to refer your consulting services to others. A strong referral network can be a powerful marketing tool.

Offering online consulting services in retirement allows you to share your wealth of knowledge and experience while maintaining flexibility and autonomy in your work. Remember to adapt and refine your approach based on the growing needs of your clients and the industry.

Afterword

It may be true that as a person who has a life-time of history in the business world, you are more experienced than the person you are working for. This can become a tricky dance to perform. Some people will consider any advice that you might offer to be coming from an underling and, therefore, not worthy of consideration. Others will disregard any tech related ideas from a person who is retired and "older" as beyond comprehension. This is the joy of ageism.

Decide what battles you want to fight. Unless you are asked for it, you may want to hold off on any sort of advice until you get the lay of the land. Does this organization, or person you are working for, prefer a "just do it because I told you to," scenario, or do they consider collaboration a bonus to the workplace? If the client does not value you, do you even want to work for them? After all, this is a part-time contract and there are many more fish in the sea, as my mother used to say about my dating life.

The role of "Virtual Assistant" could have several other labels, like Management Assistant, Executive Assistant, Research Assistant, Administrative Assistant, Personal Assistant, etc. The term "virtual" simply shows that the assistant usually works remotely, but they are probably somewhat flexible in terms of names and job description.

Regardless of the label applied to this work, it may be the most rewarding one for a retiree. This is a chance to utilize all of your experience, knowledge, dedication, work ethic, common sense, people skills and life learning. And, while we are at it, let's forget the male female thing. There is no reason whatsoever that a man cannot accept the title of "assistant" anymore than a woman can accept the title of manager, CEO, partner, director, or anything else. Time to move on folks.

This series of books, **EXTRA RETIREMENT INCOME IS SEXY**, includes many, many possibilities for retirees to add more income and enjoy more creative pursuits. Here is a brief review of the other books:

Freelance Writing: Many websites and businesses constantly need content. If you enjoy writing, you could offer your services as a freelance writer. There are platforms like Upwork and Fiverr that connect writers with clients. We will explore this opportunity in depth in book 2, **THE PROSPEROUS PEN**.

Online Tutoring: If you have expertise in a particular subject, you could offer online tutoring services. Platforms like Chegg Tutors or Wyzant allow you to connect with students seeking help. More information about online tutoring is available in book 3 of this series, **DIGITAL CLASSROOMS**.

Virtual Assistance: Many entrepreneurs and small businesses need help with tasks like email management, data entry, and scheduling. Offering virtual assistance services can be a great way to use your organizational skills. We will dive into becoming a virtual assistant in book 4, **SILVER HAIRED SAGE**.

Sell Handmade Crafts or Digital Items: If you have a talent for crafting or have accumulated unique vintage items, you can sell them on platforms like Etsy or eBay. Creating digital products like ebooks, courses and journals can lead to a world of opportunity. This exciting area of income generation is fully explained in book 5 of the series, **DESIGNING WEALTH.**

Online Surveys and Reviews: While this may not generate a substantial income, participating in online surveys can provide a small stream of income. Websites like Swagbucks or Survey Junkie offer opportunities to earn money for your opinions. Creating and sharing product reviews can lead to a very substantial income generating business. We offer all the details of this business idea in book 6, **GOLDEN INSIGHTS**.

About the Author

R obert J Bannon is still trying to define what retirement is and how to live it. Leveraging his life as an entrepreneur, sales manager, stockbroker and VP investor relations, along with 10 years as a tax consultant, Bob has written a 6 book series, EXTRA RETIREMENT INCOME IS SEXY, to help retirees create additional income and fulfillment in their life. He has also authored several other non-fiction titles, some of which are included below.

He and his wife live in the foothills of the Rockies and have 2 adult children and 3 grandsons. He continues to travel the world, play golf, and write, balanced with grocery shopping, cooking, and afternoon naps. You can reach him through his website at RobertJBannon.com.

Also By Robert J Bannon

EXTRA RETIREMENT INCOME IS SEXY
Ignite Your Financial Passion and Live the
Lifestyle You Love
BOOK 1
Paperback ISBN 978-0-9739646-9-1
Ebook ISBN 978-1-7382603-0-0

THE PROSPEROUS PEN
Mastering Freelance Writing for Retirement
Riches
Book 2
Paperback ISBN 978-1-7382603-1-7
Ebook ISBN 978-1-7382603-2-4

DIGITAL CLASSROOMS

Unlocking Retirement Riches as an Online Tutor

Book 3

Paperback ISBN 978-1-7382603-3-1

Ebook ISBN 978-1-7382603-4-8

SILVER HAIRED SAGE

Retirees Become Amazing Virtual Assistants & Increase Their Own Income

Book 4

Paperback ISBN 978-1-7382603-5-5

Ebook ISBN 978-1-7382603-6-2

DESIGNING WEALTH

A Retiree's Guide to More Income and Creative Fulfillment

Book 5

Paperback ISBN 978-1-7382603-7-9

Ebook ISBN 978-1-7382603-8-6

GOLDEN INSIGHTS

Unlocking Extra Income – A Retiree's Guide to Surveys & Reviews

Book 6

Paperback ISBN 978-1-7382603-9-3

Ebook ISBN   978-1-7382622-0-5

EASY STOCK MARKET STARTER COURSE
ASIN B09NCFC2FF   ISBN 979-8783059315

THE WEST COAST TRAIL: One Step at a Time
ASIN 172789703X   ISBN 978-1727897036

HOW TO WRITE A BOOK ABOUT WEIGHT LOSS
And any other non-fiction topic
ISBN PAPERBACK 978-1-7382622-1-2
ISBN E-BOOK   978-1-7382622-2-9

By Lonewolf Notes/RJB
ETSY SHOP MANAGER
ASIN B083XW6CXJ   ISBN 979-8601305228

MY WINE TASTING JOURNAL & NOTEBOOK
ASIN 1676781633   ISBN 978-1676781639

FINANCIAL PLANNER TEMPLATE
ASIN 1676048227   ISBN 978-1676048220